OUR JOY
PHILIPPIANS

KENNETH SCHENCK

wesleyan
publishing
house

Indianapolis, Indiana

CONTENTS

Introduction   5

Week 1: Faithful to the End   7

Week 2: One Spirit   24

Week 3: Looking toward Salvation   41

Week 4: Christ-Oriented Priorities   58

Week 5: Follow My Example   75

Week 6: Rejoicing in Gifts   92

INTRODUCTION

Philippians is one of the warmest, most encouraging letters in the New Testament—and ironically, Paul wrote it while imprisoned. It stands as a testimony to the fact that we can rejoice no matter our circumstances. The traditional view is that Paul was in Rome under house arrest during the two years mentioned in Acts 28 when he wrote this letter. However, a significant number of scholars today think Paul was in prison at Ephesus for a time on his so-called third missionary journey. If so, the situation Paul mentioned in 2 Corinthians 1:8 ("We were under great pressure, far beyond our ability to endure, so that we despaired even of life") might allude to the time when he wrote Philippians.

Whether in Rome or Ephesus, Paul was waiting to appear before Roman officials (Phil. 1:13; 4:22). It was a trial that had the potential to result in Paul's death (1:20–24). To make matters worse, he also faced opposition from other Christians who seemed eager to make things worse for him in prison (1:15–17). Paul spoke calmly about them in the first chapter, but these may also have been the Christian opponents he targeted in chapter 3.

Despite Paul's troubled situation, one of the key themes of Philippians is rejoicing, as well as Paul's desire for unity in the Philippian church. It is difficult to know exactly how many believers lived in the city, although it was probably around fifty or fewer. These Christians met in houses like that of Lydia mentioned in Acts 16:40.

The Philippian church was led by "overseers and deacons" (Phil. 1:1). It is likely that Epaphroditus, whom the Philippians entrusted with material support for Paul in prison (4:18), was one of those leaders. The Philippians had sent Epaphroditus to care for Paul, but then Epaphroditus became critically ill. When he regained enough strength to return home, Paul took the occasion to write this letter to the church and send it back with Epaphroditus (2:25–30).

Philippi itself was located north of Greece in an area known then and today as Macedonia, just a bit east of Thessalonica. After sending Epaphroditus back with the letter to the Philippian church, Paul hoped to send Timothy soon after with word of how his trial turned out (2:19–23). Paul also expected to go himself after his trial (2:24).

This book presents six weeks of Bible studies on Philippians. Each week covers a little more than half a chapter and follows a particular theme. Within each week, there are five days of reflection on the text, looking at only a few verses each day. The aim is to experience life transformation by studying the words God revealed to the Philippian church through Paul. The goal is to hear God speak to you through Scripture and then live faithfully to his Word through the power of the Holy Spirit.

FAITHFUL TO THE END

Philippians 1:1-26

"He who began a good work in you will carry it on
to completion until the day of Christ Jesus."

—PHILIPPIANS 1:6

GRACE TO YOU
Philippians 1:1-2

INTRODUCTION

Paul began Philippians with his standard greeting of "grace and peace" (1:2), and he called the Philippians "holy ones" (1:1), as he did most of the churches to which he wrote. His mention of "overseers and deacons" (1:1) was unique and gives us an indication of the way his churches were structured.

ENGAGE

Paul's greeting of "grace and peace" may very well have encapsulated his sense of mission. The standard salutation in a letter of the time was "Greetings" (*chairein*). Paul chose a related word, *grace* (*charis*), to reinforce the truth that we can only be in relationship with God because of his undeserved favor. *Peace* (*shalom*) was the standard Jewish greeting. By bringing together the Greek word *grace* and the Jewish greeting *peace*, Paul united Jew and Gentile in his greeting just as he did in his mission. Paul considered himself the apostle to non-Jews, or Gentiles, and his entire ministry was based on this calling.

EXAMINE

When Paul addressed the "overseers and deacons" (1:1) of Philippi, he gave a rare glimpse into the way his churches were structured. Paul addressed the "saints in Christ Jesus at Philippi" (1:1) rather than the church at Philippi, so it is not clear whether he was addressing one Christian assembly or many. Paul addressed Corinth, a large city where he spent many years, as a single assembly (1 Cor. 1:2), and it seems unlikely that Philippi would have significantly more churches than Corinth. The overseers and deacons of the Philippian church were leaders who took care of any service-oriented tasks. Epaphroditus was likely among these leaders and one who stood out (Phil. 2:25).

How do you think Paul's use of the word *saint* is different from the way it is used today?

"Paul and Barnabas appointed elders for them in each church and, with prayer and fasting, committed them to the Lord, in whom they had put their trust."
—ACTS 14:23

EXPLORE

All Christians are saints by God's grace. The word *saint* means "holy one," a person who belongs to God and is set apart for him. It is easy to forget the grace of God in our lives; we focus on what is going wrong or on what we do not have, and it is easy not to be at peace. But we must not just skim over this greeting Paul writes at the beginning of all his letters. God's intention for us and for our Christian leaders is grace and peace—a grace and peace that comes from our Father God and from our master, the Lord Jesus, the Christ, God's anointed one.

How is grace and peace a summary of the gospel that Paul preached?

PRAYER

Reflect on God's grace in your life, on God as your Father, and on Jesus as your Master. Do you have peace knowing you have such a Father and Lord?

BLAMELESS TO THE END

Philippians 1:3-11

INTRODUCTION

Paul set the stage for the Philippians' continued life together with Christ. They have partnered with Paul to this point, and he knew that God would be faithful to them until the end. He prayed for them to continue blamelessly until Christ's return.

ENGAGE

Paul was absolutely confident in the faithfulness of God. God began a good work in the Philippian church, and he would be faithful to carry it through to the end. At the same time, Paul was convinced that God's grace required our faithful response. We cannot earn God's favor, but he expects us to respond appropriately to the gift of grace he gives us. By his power, we can and must meet his grace with a blameless life and with the fruit of righteousness. God can help us to "discern what is best" (1:10) so that we live pure and blameless lives.

Where we are in the journey is not nearly so important as the fact that we are still on it and still traveling with God.

EXAMINE

These verses have a personal tone because they begin the "thanksgiving" section of Paul's letter, an element in ancient letters that broke the ice between the letter writer and his recipient. Paul referred to his history with the church in proclaiming God's good news. He spoke of his joy over them and the fact that they shared God's grace. He spoke of his longing for them. He also anticipated the future when they would increase their knowledge and discernment. He looked forward to the day of Christ's return from heaven and prayed Christ would find them blameless. He prayed they would be found having an abundance of righteousness for Christ to see in their lives when he returned.

Why do you think discernment is such an important concern when it comes to living out the gospel?

EXPLORE

These verses give a wonderful picture for churches today to imitate. It is a picture of a local church faithful in the past, present, and future. Would it not be great if our church had a legacy of joy, grace, and doing God's work in the world together? Would it not be wonderful to see our pastors and church leaders longing to progress? Would it not be great if we all expected our communities of faith to be found blameless at the time of Christ's return, with obvious "fruit of righteousness" (1:11) to show? It can happen by God's grace!

Do you think churches today have the same expectations that Paul had for the churches he planted? Why or why not?

PRAYER

Father, I know that you are always faithful to complete what you begin. May I also be faithful to the end—to the day of my death or Christ's return.

THE GOSPEL WILL ADVANCE

Philippians 1:12-14

INTRODUCTION

From a human standpoint, Paul's imprisonment seemed like a setback. But God can advance his good news even through opposition.

ENGAGE

Paul mentioned two ways in which his imprisonment advanced the gospel. First, he was able to share the gospel with the palace guard. They would not have heard the good news if Paul had not been arrested. Second, his chains had a positive effect on the Christian community. Paul faced what were likely some of their greatest fears—and he maintained his joy and faith. This gave others the courage to proclaim the good news of Jesus without fear of the consequences. Paul's experiences showed that the things that seem like defeats and setbacks can be another way to advance the gospel.

EXAMINE

In the Roman world, prison was mostly reserved for those who could not repay their debts; a crime was punished with a fine or exile. It is likely that Paul was waiting to appear before a Roman official: the Roman governor of Ephesus or Nero. Regardless of where Paul was, his chains did not stop him from sharing the gospel, even among those guarding him.

Why do you think Paul wanted the Philippian church to know the benefits of his imprisonment for the gospel?

Christ will find a way. In fact, he *is* the way.

EXPLORE

It took some doing, but Paul reminded his readers that God can take a difficult situation, like imprisonment, and bring good out of it. We do not have to like hardship, but we can benefit by adopting Paul's attitude. Our mission does not stop when we face challenges and obstacles. These are opportunities for ministry. Paul's example reminds us that others are watching us. We do not succeed or fail as individual Christians; actions impact the lives of the people around us.

Think about all the people with whom you interact on a daily basis. How have your recent reactions to challenging circumstances displayed the gospel? How have they not?

PRAYER

Lord, help me to put the challenges of my life in perspective. Help me to see them as opportunities rather than obstacles and to take comfort from your example in having peace and joy through suffering.

ONE WAY OR ANOTHER
Philippians 1:15-18

INTRODUCTION

Christians continued to preach the gospel during Paul's imprisonment, which made him a focus of Roman interest. Some did it knowing Paul wanted the opportunity to present the gospel to Roman leaders. Others hoped it would get him in more trouble. Either way, the gospel was preached.

ENGAGE

You see it in war. You see it in a mob. You see it in politics and the judicial system. When you have someone who represents a situation otherwise out of control, you tend to pin your frustration on that person. Similarly, the preaching of the gospel outside Paul's prison had the potential to cause huge problems for him. The Romans could have made an example of him. Rather than round up everyone, they could have given Paul such a harsh punishment that everyone else would have gotten the message. Paul seemed aware of this fact, but he did not look at the situation with despair. Rather, he rejoiced that the gospel was getting such incredible publicity.

EXAMINE

We sometimes think that everyone in the early church believed and taught the same things. In reality, they disagreed over a number of issues. Paul faced opposition for the way he blurred the lines between Jew and Gentile and ignored the purity laws that distinguished Jews from Gentiles. In this case, Paul saw these individuals as preaching the gospel insincerely. Perhaps they emphasized how different Paul's approach was from theirs and tried to make him look like a trouble-maker. Although there may have been some differences, they must have preached that Jesus died for sins and rose from the dead, or else Paul would not have rejoiced in the good news they brought.

What are some examples today where people are preaching Jesus' death and resurrection but may have some theological differences? Should we rejoice in the same way Paul did?

EXPLORE

It is especially hard for us to rejoice in the good that is sometimes done through people whose motives we question—especially when they are causing us problems personally. The level of self-denial that Paul demonstrated is extremely difficult to reach. We want the truth to be known about our opponents. We want their true motives exposed. How incredibly patient God must be! He knows all the impure motives and intentions, and yet he bears with them for now. He brings good through evil people. He brings good through individuals he will later judge. What a difficult model for us to follow! Can we rejoice in the good that comes through unjust people when we do not have the power to expose their insincerity?

Why do you think Paul was able to rejoice in the ministry of those who, from his perspective, were preaching the gospel insincerely? How can we emulate this in our own lives?

Don't worry about sorting out the motives of others.
That's God's business, and he's very good at it.

PRAYER

Spirit, give me the strength to submit to your timing. Give me the patience to persevere through personal trials that I may serve you.

TO LIVE IS CHRIST
Philippians 1:19-26

INTRODUCTION

Paul wrestled with his immediate fate. Would the Romans put him to death, or would he survive to continue his ministry? He was convinced he would survive and continue for the progress of the Philippians' faith.

ENGAGE

Paul had faith he would be released. It is clear from what he said in this section that he was facing a possible death sentence from the Roman government. It is possible that 2 Corinthians 1:9 referred to this time when he felt as if he had a potential "sentence of death" hanging over him. He was ready to either live or die. The Spirit of Christ and the prayers of the Philippians convinced him he would not be condemned to death.

EXAMINE

These verses provide a rare glimpse into Paul's understanding of what happens to Christians between death and the resurrection of our bodies when Christ returns. Paul said that we die and go to be with Christ. While most Christians take this idea for granted—that we are awake somewhere between our death and resurrection—we only find hints of it in Paul's writings, in Philippians 1:19–26 and in 2 Corinthians 5:8. In fact, Paul uses the word *sleep* in reference to our intermediate state in the earlier letters of 1 Thessalonians and 1 Corinthians, leading scholars to wonder if Paul's thinking on the subject developed in the meantime.

What is the practical significance to believers regarding what happens between death and resurrection?

> "Those who have a 'why' to live, can bear
> with almost any 'how.'"
> —VIKTOR FRANKL

EXPLORE

We cannot always count on being delivered from our hardships. Hebrews 11:35 tells of those who showed faith leading to deliverance and those who showed faith to the death. Along with Paul, they modeled the appropriate attitude in all situations. Those who have near-death experiences or who face a terminal illness frequently find themselves with a clear sense of what is and is not important. Even getting that room clean, the scratch someone gave your fender before leaving the parking lot, the snide comment your spouse made—these things really do not have much eternal significance. Family, relationships, God— these sorts of things are truly valuable and should be the focus of our energies.

How do you think Paul's comments in this passage relate to his frequent observation that he was a "[servant] of Christ Jesus" (Phil. 1:1)?

PRAYER

Father, help me to focus my eyes on what is eternal and lasting. Give me the strength to keep my eyes fixed on you whether I live or die.

BRIDGING PAUL'S WORLD AND OURS

Every once in a while, we tend to stop and take stock of our lives. When we're young, we often think we have an unlimited amount of time left to do anything we want. Then we walk through a number of significant choices. We may get married. Perhaps we have children. We may get a job and start a career. Time begins to speed by; our bodies begin to rebel against us. We no longer think anything is possible. Sometimes we may feel trapped, like we're headed nowhere. Most people eventually come to a point of questioning, a moment of self-doubt, or a dawning realization. We may wonder if we made the right choices.

In times like these, Paul's promise to the Philippians can take on meaning: "he who began a good work in you will carry it on to completion" (1:6). Paul said these words in the difficult situation of being wrongly imprisoned. His words remind us that God is in control of our lives. He is leading us toward his kingdom. This is a great promise—we have an incredible destination no matter how we may feel at this particular moment.

EXERCISE

Reflect on Philippians 1:21: "For to me, to live is Christ and to die is gain." List some elements of your life that feel like death to you. Now reflect on Christ as life. Give each of the "death" items to Christ and rejoice in living for him.

ONE SPIRIT

Philippians 1:27 – 2:11

"Whatever happens, conduct yourselves in a manner worthy
of the gospel of Christ. Then, whether I come and see
you or only hear about you in my absence,
I will know that you stand firm in one spirit."

—PHILIPPIANS 1:27

ONE SPIRIT AND SOUL
Philippians 1:27-28

INTRODUCTION

These verses show us a key characteristic of a community that strives to be faithful to the gospel: It will have unity in its spirit and soul.

ENGAGE

The NIV translation highlights the fact that Paul spoke of the community needing to have "one spirit" (1:27). Similarly, the NIV says the community should contend for faith as "one man" (1:27), as if they were a single individual. The literal translation means "one soul." Both images—one spirit and one soul—highlight the degree of unity to which Paul was aiming in the Philippian church. When believers have this unity, it is a sign of the salvation by and indwelling of God—we have the unity of God inside us.

"Make us one, Lord, make us one . . .
We belong together. We are family."
—MALDWYN POPE

EXAMINE

After finishing the thanksgiving section of the letter, Paul moved on to the body of the letter. He began with one of the two key themes of Philippians: the unity of the Christian community. Later in the letter we will read of two of Paul's former female coworkers, Euodia and Syntyche, who were having trouble agreeing with each other. We do not know the extent of such disagreements in the church at Philippi. In general, this assembly of God at Philippi at least seemed to be more tightly knit than the one at Corinth. The Greek word Paul used when he told them to conduct themselves this way (*politeuomai*) was generally used of those who live as responsible citizens of a city or state.

Why do you think Paul was so concerned about the unity of the church?

EXPLORE

Can you imagine how unified churches would be if they contended for faith as if they were a single individual? We all have moments where we cannot make up our mind between different courses of action, but we would not normally harm ourselves or do things that would hurt some part of our body. What a powerful picture of a local church—a single individual walking with God. What the church is contending for is "the faith of the gospel" (1:27). Paul was not referring to a set of ideas here, but faithfulness to the good news, just as he had said to walk worthy of the gospel. We once again have Paul's consistent expectation that Christian lives would be marked by faithfulness.

What do you think a church would look like that is contending for faithfulness to the gospel as one body?

PRAYER

Spirit, give me the unity of mind and heart that I want but find so hard to attain. When I do not desire it, bend my will to desire it. Help me to work in community in such a way that we will be seen as one body striving for your goals.

PRIVILEGE OF SUFFERING
Philippians 1:29-30

INTRODUCTION

Paul explained that it is a privilege to believe in Christ—something we do not always remember. But Paul also told the Philippians that it is a privilege to suffer for Christ!

ENGAGE

Paul consistently modeled throughout Philippians that we should be thankful not only for experiences we identify as good, but also those we think of as bad. Believing is certainly a privilege. It might not always occur to us that it is a privilege to have faith, but once Paul pointed it out, it made sense. It is hard for us to see suffering for Christ as a gift and privilege. Apparently, the Philippians were experiencing some of the same hardships for their faith that they had seen Paul undergo. Paul indicated that such hardships were also a privilege for believers. Hardships serve as our connection not only to Paul and other Christians who suffered, but also to Jesus.

> "Consider it pure joy, my brothers, whenever you face trials of many kinds, because you know that the testing of your faith develops perseverance."
> —JAMES 1:2–3

EXAMINE

The Greek word Paul used to speak of the privilege of suffering for Christ (*pascho*) had the connotation of grace as a gift from God. In a world oriented around honor and shame, Paul said it was an honor to both believe and suffer for Christ. Paul sometimes used the language of election, of God choosing us, in his writings. Such language emphasizes God's control over the world and his favor toward believers. However, this language for Paul did not mean that only certain people could be saved or that those chosen could not fail to be saved. What it affirms is the honor of serving God in stronger terms than intellectual propositions could capture.

Can you think of other situations where it is considered an honor to serve? To suffer? How is it even more of an honor to suffer for Christ?

EXPLORE

Christians often mistake faith for something we can do under our own power. Historically, Christianity has not looked at faith this way. Even John Wesley saw faith as something God had to give us, something God empowered us to have through his Holy Spirit. God gives us all the power to respond at some point in our lives, but the timing is not of our choosing. Herein is the danger of refusing or turning from God when he offers. God is merciful, but it is hardly worth chancing an outcome like Esau's, described in Hebrews 12:16–17. He could not find it within himself to repent, even though he realized what was at stake.

PRAYER

Father, lead me to respond when you call. Give me a spirit of thankfulness, not only for faith, but for the privilege to suffer for you.

OTHERS FIRST

Philippians 2:1-4

INTRODUCTION

Paul continued the theme of being in one spirit by urging the Philippians to think not only of themselves, but also about the needs and desires of others. This, he said, was one sure way to encourage him in his trials.

ENGAGE

When Jesus was asked to boil down all of God's requirements into a single command, he brought them all down to two: love God and love your neighbor. His teaching makes it clear that he included everyone in the neighbor category, including enemies. So, Paul extended this basic Christian ethic into the relationships of the Philippians. They were to think about others and not just themselves. They were not to strive against each other or do things just to earn glory for themselves. If they really wanted to encourage Paul and one another in such times of trial, here was the way: Love God and others. This was the path to encouragement, comfort, compassion, and mercy.

EXAMINE

Paul spoke just a few verses earlier of being of "one spirit" and "one man" (1:27). Here, he used yet another Greek word (*sympsykos*) that means something like "one spirit and purpose" (2:2). Paul wished them to have "the same love" (2:2), to think the same. These are all different ways of saying the same thing: Believers are to love and treat others as if they were themselves. A person of sound mind would never hurt or cut off parts of his or her body (see 1 Cor. 12:14–26). We are to nurture each other like we would ourselves.

What do you think it would look like for people to consider others better than themselves?

"The eye cannot say to the hand, 'I don't need you!'
And the head cannot say to the feet, 'I don't need you!'"
—1 Corinthians 12:21

EXPLORE

The default human mode is to take care of oneself first. We would expect the church to be different, but too often it is not. The idea that we are all part of the body of Jesus is not a new thought to most of us. We have heard it so often that we are inoculated against its impact. The problem is not that we do not know we are to be unified or to love each other, but rather that we have failed so regularly and thoroughly that we have despaired of success and decided to ignore this truth.

How can the church operate more like the body of Christ?

PRAYER

Spirit, prove me wrong in my doubts so that I can truly love others and be united in spirit and actions with them. Soften my hardened heart.

THINKING LIKE JESUS

Philippians 2:5-8

INTRODUCTION

Paul told the Philippians to have the same attitude toward each other that Jesus showed toward us. He not only emptied himself of his divine privileges and became a servant, but he was even willing to die on a cross for us.

ENGAGE

The traditional Christian reading of this poem sees three phases of Christ's existence in it. The first stanza (2:6–7) is connected to Christ's preexistence before he took on human flesh. Although he existed in the "form of God" (NRSV), he did not exploit this status, but instead adopted the status of a servant. The second stanza (2:7–8) speaks of the incarnated Christ humbling himself to the most degrading form of death at the time—crucifixion. Then the final stanza (2:9–11) speaks of his subsequent exaltation by God the Father to king of the cosmos. Today, we will focus on the first two stanzas (2:6–8), which explain that we should have the same servant attitude that Jesus demonstrated.

EXAMINE

This poem is often called the Philippian hymn because at least the first four verses have a fairly clear poetic rhythm. Paul also inserted comments like "even death on a cross!" (2:8) and "to the glory of God the Father" (2:11), which may imply that he did not actually write this poem or hymn himself. The first stanza is usually understood as referring to Christ's incarnation, the preexistent Christ emptying himself of the authority of his divinity and becoming human. The second stanza then tells of Jesus as a human humbling himself to the point of being willing to die on a cross. Throughout these first two stanzas, the poem emphasizes Jesus' focus on servanthood and willingness to relinquish his privileged status.

Why do you think Paul might have chosen to include a quote from a hymn or poem rather than writing his own thoughts?

EXPLORE

The comparison here between Jesus and us is so startling that some scholars have tried to explain it away. Surely we cannot actually be like Jesus—he was so selfless, so humble. But this is exactly the message Paul gave to the Philippians. They were to have the same mind of servanthood that Jesus had. Yes, they must be willing to lower themselves in the service of others as much as a servant is lower than a king, as much as humanity is lower than Christ's divinity. Most of us never have much status of which to empty ourselves. If we gain it, we take advantage of it. Jesus had a status far higher than any of us will ever have, and he gave it away.

What examples have you seen of people humbling themselves or giving away their statuses?

No one could possibly stoop lower to serve
another than Christ stooped to serve us.

PRAYER

Father, in obedience to you, may I not only be a servant to my brothers and sisters, but may I fully recognize my humble state before you.

JESUS IS LORD!

Philippians 2:9-11

INTRODUCTION

While the first part of the Philippian poem recounts Christ's descent and obedient humbling of himself, the final section tells of how God exalted him as Lord of all creation in response.

ENGAGE

The first part of the hymn showed us Jesus as a model of self-sacrifice and humility. We of course cannot imitate the final stanza entirely, where God exalts Jesus as Lord over all creation. The main takeaway we should have from this final part is to recognize that Jesus is our Lord and, indeed, those who resist his lordship today will one day bow before him. We participate more in the exaltation of Jesus than we might think at first. Just as God raised Jesus from the dead, he will also raise us, after death and even in this life (see 2 Cor. 4:14; Rom. 6:4). And we will ultimately reign with Christ as well (2 Tim. 2:11–12).

EXAMINE

This final stanza begins with the word *therefore*, which tells us that God exalted Jesus in response to his obedience to the point of death, in response to the faithfulness of Jesus (see Heb. 5:7; Rom. 5:19). Jesus takes on the name Lord. We see this sequence in other New Testament passages where it is foretold that Jesus will be given the role of king of the universe at the point of his resurrection and exaltation to God's right hand (see Acts 2:36; 13:33; Rom. 10:9; Heb. 1:4–5). The hymn alludes to Isaiah 45:23, perhaps the Old Testament passage that most emphasizes that God is the only true God.

What are some of the real-life implications of Paul's proclamation that Jesus is Lord?

"I am the LORD, and there is no other; apart from me there is no God. . . . Before me every knee will bow; by me every tongue will swear."
—ISAIAH 45:5, 23

EXPLORE

Christians can sometimes focus so much on Jesus' divinity that they forget that he was fully human as well. If we could flash back two thousand years, we might conclude that the earliest Christians did the opposite. They knew Jesus was human; they had seen him. They also knew that in his resurrection, he far surpassed any human they had ever known. Today, we run the risk of missing how much Jesus identified with our human limitations. He became lower than the angels and was truly tempted, and his obedience required effort, just as it does for us.

Why is it difficult for us to grasp that Jesus was a human being?

PRAYER

Lord Jesus, help me to confess with my mouth and believe with my heart that you are Lord so that I may use my life to fully submit to your lordship.

BRIDGING PAUL'S WORLD AND OURS

In world politics, we often see leaders earn their riches through corrupt means. The countries of the world are rife with bribery, rigged elections, stolen international aid, and other tricks that make those in power richer while their citizens get poorer. Eventually, someone rises up and overthrows the corrupt leader. The interesting thing is that the very people who overthrew the previous tyrant will often fall into exactly the same way of living.

Jesus tells his disciples in Mark 10:42–45 that they are not to be like the typical rulers of the nations. They are not to hold it over others, but they must become servants, just as Jesus came to serve. This is the attitude the Philippian hymn portrays vividly in Jesus, and it is the attitude that Paul urged the Philippians to have toward one another. Christians are to lead and relate to others as servants, working for the good of others.

EXERCISE

For the next twenty-four hours, examine every decision you make that has an impact on someone else around you. As you make the decision, picture yourself on the receiving end of the decision. How would you choose if you were the other person?

LOOKING TOWARD SALVATION
Philippians 2:12-30

"Continue to work out your salvation with fear and trembling, for it is God who works in you to will and to act according to his good purpose."

—PHILIPPIANS 2:12–13

DAY 1

WORK OUT SALVATION TOGETHER
Philippians 2:12-13

INTRODUCTION

Paul realized that he would not always be around to give answers. He urged the Philippian community to move toward the goal of final salvation and to be aware of the guiding presence of God.

ENGAGE

Sometimes, we emphasize the central role of God's grace and faith so much that we miss the clear place that working plays in salvation. In these verses, Paul said that it would take some effort on our part to make it across the finish line of salvation. Salvation is in the future—the judgment has not yet come, so we have not yet escaped it. Paul consistently indicated that, as unlikely as it may be, it was possible that even he might not make it if he did not continue striving (see 1 Cor. 9:26–27;

Phil. 3:11). These verses speak of the collective effort that we make together as a community of faith to make it to the finish line. Together, we are to "work out" (2:12) our very salvation.

"God works in you; therefore, you can work; otherwise it would be impossible."
—JOHN WESLEY

EXAMINE

To Paul, *salvation* referred to being rescued from the wrathful judgment of God. Paul never claimed a precise date, and in the early days of his ministry, he probably expected it to happen within his lifetime. But as he aged, it appears he seemed to sense that he would die before Christ's return. He would not be able to solve all the problems of his churches directly. He would have to let go and trust God to work in the hearts of his congregations.

In what ways do we need to continue to work out our salvation? What are some ways we can do that?

EXPLORE

It is hard for many of us to leave important things to God, let alone to other human beings. It is often hard for us to let go of our children, even when the law says they have come of age. It is often not enough for us to tell others how we think they should live; we also have the impulse to police our instruction. We want to force others to follow through, to catch and punish the secret sin. Do we not truly believe God sees it all? Why do we think we have to do his business? In the end, we cannot. At some point, we have to leave it up to God and allow others to stand on their own before him.

Where is the balance between being concerned for others and leaving them to make their own way through life?

PRAYER

Father, empower me to trust your work in me and among the members of my congregation. Give me faith that your kingdom will always find its way on earth, as in heaven.

STOP ARGUING

Philippians 2:14-15

INTRODUCTION

Some of the Philippians were grumbling and arguing. Paul told them they must stop if they were to stand out as shining lights in their world, as well as if they wanted to be without fault in God's eyes.

ENGAGE

Paul did not have absolute perfection in mind when he spoke of being without blame or fault before God. In that case, blamelessness was as simple as stopping the bickering some of them were doing. He was probably thinking at least about Euodia and Syntyche, two women who worked with him when he was in Philippi previously. We know they had some conflict (4:2–3). Paul assumed that not only can such individuals stop their bickering, but they must stop in order to be blameless before God. Christians are supposed to look strikingly different from the world around them. Believers are supposed to shine like stars in their unity and love in a "crooked and depraved" (2:14) world.

EXAMINE

This is the second time in the letter (see also 1:10) that Paul casually mentioned his expectation that the Philippians would be blameless. The verses that follow make it clear he was thinking about the day of Christ's return. Philippians 2:15 actually uses three different words for the same thing: *blameless*, *pure*, and *without fault*. Though we may rarely think about it today, it was clearly a major point in Paul's mind. Another point where Paul differed from the current spirit of the age was to see Christians as shining stars in contrast to the world around them. The current focus is to see ourselves as mostly like everyone else, even to the degree that we see it as a virtue to blend in. Paul did not agree.

In what ways should Christians be different from the world around them so they can "shine like stars" (2:15)?

EXPLORE

No one who has been in the church for long will have trouble understanding what Paul was talking about here. Complaining and arguing, unfortunately, seem to be common characteristics of churches throughout time. We know we shouldn't do it—almost anyone would tell you that. Yet it happens so frequently, and we seem to feel little guilt about it. We sometimes even justify it, hiding behind the "legitimacy" of our complaints or standing up for the truth. In the end, complaining usually only makes us feel better; it does not solve anything.

Why do you think the church has historically put up with certain sins like complaining and arguing? What can we do about this?

> "Those who are never at fault in what they say are perfect,
> able to keep their whole body in check."
> —JAMES 3:2 (TNIV)

PRAYER

Spirit, expose my excuses for doing things I know deep down I should not do. Provide people in my life to gently show me my true motives.

SOMETHING TO TALK ABOUT

Philippians 2:16-18

INTRODUCTION

Paul looked forward to the honor the Philippians would bring him on the day of Christ. Even the thought of being able to present them to God as the fruit of his labor made the offering of his life worth it.

ENGAGE

Paul continued the thought of the previous verse by telling us how the Philippians might shine like stars in the world (2:16), namely, in the way they demonstrate to the world the "word of life." The word of life was the offer of salvation through Jesus Christ, the possibility of escaping God's righteous judgment of the world. Paul had no fear or expectation that his efforts on behalf of the Philippians would turn out to be pointless. He had run a strenuous race for them. He had worked hard as an apostle. When the Philippians would stand blameless before God, Paul would have seen that his hard work was truly worth it.

EXAMINE

In both ancient Israel and the ancient world in general, those offering a sacrifice sometimes poured a drink offering on top of what they had already offered. Paul used this imagery in 2:17. The faithfulness of the Philippians was already a sacrifice to God, an act of sacrificial worship (the word the NIV translates as "service"). Paul could have thought of his own self-sacrifice as part of the same offering the Philippians were making to God with their own lives. So they could have rejoiced together in their mutual offering. The Greek word for *faith* had several possible nuances, one of which was faithfulness. The "faith" Paul had in mind was not likely their mere belief in Christ but their faith*fulness*.

Who are the people in your life that, like Paul with the Philippians, can rejoice in your faithfulness to Christ? Pray a prayer of thanksgiving for them.

"He is no fool who gives what he cannot keep
to gain what he cannot lose."
—JIM ELLIOT

EXPLORE

Much of Paul's thinking here may seem foreign, even objectionable to us today. He put an incredible emphasis on effort, working, and faithfulness. He used categories of honor and reward positively. He wanted to have something to boast about on the day of Christ. The Philippians were shining stars in a depraved world. His work might have been in vain if the Philippians did not make it to the end. Even so, Paul would no doubt agree to add an important footnote to these sorts of informal comments: by God's grace. It is by God's grace that we can make this effort. Our boasting is in the context of gifts from God that are completely disproportionate to anything we might do.

PRAYER

Father, thank you for honors and rewards we could never truly earn, for the privilege of offering ourselves on an altar of worship to you.

TIMOTHY WILL COME

Philippians 2:19-24

INTRODUCTION

Paul prepared the way for his coworker, Timothy, to visit the Philippians just as soon as Paul's verdict was given. Eventually, Paul hoped to visit the Philippians himself. In the meantime, he vouched for Timothy's character.

ENGAGE

We catch a glimpse of Paul's close relationship to Timothy in these verses. So many of those around him, Paul said, were only out for their own interests. He mentioned some of them previously (1:17). Not so with Timothy. Paul thought of him like a son. Timothy's concern for the Philippians mirrored Paul's concern for them. Just as Paul was confident in his administration of the gospel, so he was confident to send Timothy to represent him. Scholars do not know exactly how many years the two had been ministering together by this time. It may only have been about ten years. Nevertheless, they had covered an immense amount of ground together in that decade.

> "A friend is another self."
> —Latin proverb

EXAMINE

Paul likely planned to send this letter to the Philippians by way of a man from Philippi named Epaphroditus. But Paul knew that the Philippians were also deeply concerned to hear of the outcome of his trial. He then made plans to send Timothy with news as soon as the verdict was made. Then Paul hoped to come as well. Acts 19–20 tell us that after Paul's ordeal in Ephesus, he did indeed arrange his travel plans to go through Philippi on his way to Corinth.

Who in your life plays the role of Paul? Who can you mentor as your Timothy?

EXPLORE

The older we get, the more we recognize the value of someone who will protect our interests when it does not affect them or even when it is to their disadvantage. Timothy was such a person for Paul. Paul could count on him even when he was completely helpless in prison. But their partnership went beyond friendship or even a kind of family relationship. They were partners in the mission of God to save the world. Paul could not only trust Timothy with personal matters, but he could also trust him with divine matters. God may call some of us to be Pauls in this world, but he might also call some of us to be Timothys, to become partners with other leaders in carrying out God's mission.

Do you see yourself more as a Paul or a Timothy?

PRAYER

Christ, you are both my Lord and my brother. Give me partners in ministry with whom I can be either a parent or a child.

SENDING EPAPHRODITUS
Philippians 2:25-30

INTRODUCTION

The Philippians had sent aid to Paul with a man named Epaphroditus who almost died. Now, Paul sent Epaphroditus back to gladden their hearts, probably with the letter of Philippians itself.

ENGAGE

Some scholars have suggested that the trigger for writing Philippians in the first place was Paul's gratitude for the material support they sent him while he was in prison, although he was careful not to get entangled in the strings such gifts could bring (see 4:11). The church sent the material help at the hands of one of their leaders, a man named Epaphroditus. While he was with Paul, however, he became deathly ill, which brought great concern to the Philippians when they heard the news. Paul sent him back to encourage the Philippians. All in all, it is a wonderful story of Christians behaving as they should, caring for and helping each other.

> "We want you to know about the grace that God has given
> the Macedonian churches. Out of the most severe trial,
> their overflowing joy and their extreme poverty
> welled up in rich generosity."
> —2 CORINTHIANS 8:1–2

EXAMINE

It was necessary for those imprisoned in the Roman world to find individuals on the outside to feed and support them. When the Philippians heard of Paul's imprisonment, they sent one of their leaders with material support. But Paul walked a fine line in this text and later in Philippians 4. Receiving such support usually came with strings attached and brought with it a sense of owing the benefactor something later. Paul deflected these aspects of giving. He spoke of their gift as fulfilling an obligation they already had toward him (2:30). He did not exactly thank them directly, and he spoke of sending Epaphroditus back almost as a gift to them (2:28).

Why do you think it was important for Paul to avoid owing something to the Philippians or anyone who had helped him?

EXPLORE

This brief glimpse into the relationships of some early believers gives us a model for how Christian communities can help each other today. The Philippians saw Paul's need from afar. In response, they did more than pray. They mobilized their resources, even though they were likely a poor community (see 2 Cor. 8:2). They sent a mission team in the person of Epaphroditus. Paul repaid their concern, showing concern for Epaphroditus when he was ill and the emotional health of the Philippians. This vignette models the one spirit and mind that Paul had already urged several times in the letter up to this point. It is a story to which we can immediately relate and one we should strive to replicate.

How have you experienced such Christian community?

PRAYER

Spirit, give our churches this concern for one another, not only in our words but in our deeds, and not only when we are overflowing but also when it takes sacrifice.

BRIDGING PAUL'S WORLD AND OURS

Christian thinkers have gone around and around about the paradoxes of waiting for God and stepping out in faith, of us working and God working. An old preacher's story tells of a man sitting on the roof of his house waiting to be rescued from the rising waters of a flood. But he passes up several possibilities waiting for the specific kind of rescue he wants. We do not always recognize or prefer the ways that God works, but he is working.

Another common image on this issue is the "voice behind you" of Isaiah 30:21, the idea that God will correct your path when you start to deviate from his. This passage from Philippians 2 presents a similar approach. We will not know for sure this side of the kingdom what the precise equation of God and us working is, but we move forward together, not as individuals. We pray and do our best to discern God's will in particular circumstances, sometimes to wait, sometimes to move forward. God works in us to help us make those decisions, and when we go astray, God will bring a course correction.

EXERCISE

Reflect on two major decisions your church has made in the last five years. Can you discern God's hand in the decision? If it was a bad choice, did someone hear God's voice? If it was a good choice, was there a peace that God was working in the community?

CHRIST-ORIENTED PRIORITIES
Philippians 3:1-16

"But whatever was to my profit I now consider loss for
the sake of Christ . . . compared to the surpassing
greatness of knowing Christ Jesus my Lord,
for whose sake I have lost all things."

—PHILIPPIANS 3:7–8

SPIRITUALLY BRANDED

Philippians 3:1-3

INTRODUCTION

Paul started the final part of his letter with a warning not to listen to some of those dissenters who caused him problems elsewhere in the church, particularly with the Galatians. He emphasized that it is not physical circumcision that counts, but worship through the Spirit.

ENGAGE

This section begins with encouragement to rejoice in the Lord—an intriguing exhortation knowing that Paul himself was in prison and the Philippians were also undergoing hardships. (He picked this thread of thought back up in chapter 4.) In the meantime, Paul stopped to warn the Philippians not to be led astray by Christians who taught non-Jews that they must be circumcised and fully convert to Judaism in order to escape God's coming wrath. Philippians does not have extended arguments like the books of Romans and Galatians over what it means to be in right standing with God, but Paul did stop long enough to warn them that God is not interested in the branding of their flesh but in the worship of their spirit.

EXAMINE

It is rarely a compliment in any culture to call someone a dog. A Jew might insult a non-Jewish male by calling him a dog. Like a dog, a Gentile man is uncircumcised. It is deeply ironic that Paul called the Judaizers who insisted you could not be saved unless you became circumcised "dogs" (3:2). Paul also called them "mutilators [*katatom*] of the flesh" (3:2), playing on the word *circumcision* (*peritom*). It is important to recognize that these people were believers in Jesus like Paul, like the Pharisees who believed in Jesus in Acts 15:5, but Paul did not agree with them (see Gal. 2:4).

What does Paul's language tell you about his deep feelings and concern over this issue?

EXPLORE

It may seem obvious that Paul was right and his opponents wrong. Believers know God is interested in spiritual worship, not some branding of the foreskin. But if we really want to learn from this story, we need to realize that the right answer was not nearly as obvious at the time. Both sides were fully convinced they were right. Sometimes it does matter to God what we do with our flesh—the Christian life is hardly just a matter of our spirits. And it is sobering to realize that there are likely some issues we are absolutely convinced of that we are actually quite wrong.

What can we learn from the disagreements in the early church about how we should approach disagreements in our churches today?

"A man is not a Jew if he is only one outwardly, nor is circumcision merely outward and physical. No, a man is a Jew if he is one inwardly; and circumcision is circumcision of the heart, by the Spirit, not by the written code."
—ROMANS 2:28–29

PRAYER

Spirit, help me focus most on the spiritual things, while recognizing that God is interested in my entire being, and make me humble so that I can realize the limitations of my understanding.

DAY 2

AN EARTHLY RESUME
Philippians 3:4-6

INTRODUCTION

Paul argued that he could play the same game as his Judaizing opponents if it were the right game. He had all the characteristics to make him a righteous Israelite, if that was what was really important.

ENGAGE

If earthly qualifications were important, Paul had them. He was circumcised in the appropriate way. He was born a Jew and could identify his tribe. He spoke Aramaic, even though he was born in the Diaspora. Any biases a purist might have had against the Greek-speaking Jews scattered throughout the world did not apply to him. He was a Pharisee, one of the strictest sects within Judaism at the time. At one time, Paul must have scrupulously followed the oral traditions of the elders on how to keep the Law. He even persecuted Christians before he believed. Most startlingly of all, Paul said he was blameless as much as anyone could be in keeping the Jewish Law.

> "Naked I came from my mother's womb, and naked
> I will depart. The LORD gave and the LORD has taken
> away; may the name of the LORD be praised."
> —JOB 1:21

EXAMINE

Paul's statement that he was blameless, "as to righteousness under the law" (NRSV) is quite eye-opening. Many Christians picture Paul as someone whose sense of moral failure and inability to live righteously finally led him to discover the doctrine of justification by faith—that a person can only become right with God by an act of trust. As true as justification by faith is, Paul gave no real evidence in his writings of this sort of pre-faith struggle. He described himself as faultless in his law-keeping. In general, Paul was probably more like the Pharisee of Luke 18:9–14 before his conversion than the self-conflicted introspective he is often pictured to be.

What do you think Paul meant when he said that he was blameless with regard to the law? Does this imply perfect obedience? Give reasons for your answer.

EXPLORE

It is not that God does not value our efforts to be good before we come to faith. Indeed, it would seem that God empowers unbelieving humans all over the world to do good things. The point we learn from Paul is that what we do is simply not what God is looking for, nor does any amount of goodness we do offset the fact that we are all unrighteous. God has chosen to reconcile the world to himself through Jesus Christ. More importantly, we learn from Paul that our human résumés simply do not matter against eternity. It is Christ that is significant— and our faith in him is the truly important item to have on our eternal résumé.

What are some ways people today tend to trust in their own achievements?

PRAYER

Lord Jesus, plant in my heart what I already know with my head— that where or to whom I was born does not matter. And neither do my accomplishments; the only thing that matters is my faith in you.

WHAT REALLY COUNTS
Philippians 3:7-9

INTRODUCTION

Paul put his former status as a law-observant Jew into proper perspective. Things on his résumé that he might have boasted about on a human level were nothing when put next to the vast excellence of knowing Christ. What really mattered was that he was found in Christ.

ENGAGE

These verses present a contrast between all Paul's accomplishments and the surpassing excellence of Christ. His achievements were rubbish next to the possibility of knowing Christ. They were things he gladly discarded in order to be found in Christ. Paul was willing to lose everything on the human plane in order to participate in Christ's coming kingdom and the coming resurrection. To be found in Christ is to be incorporated into his faithful death, to die with Christ so that we might one day also be raised with him (see Rom. 6:4–5). To be identified with Christ in this way is what really counts!

EXAMINE

Philippians 3:9 gives just the smallest glimpse of issues that are more fully discussed in the books of Romans and Galatians. What counts as righteousness before God? Paul mentioned that he was blameless as far as the righteousness you could have by keeping the Jewish Law. But apparently God was looking for a different kind of righteousness. God looked to the righteous death of Jesus rather than to our righteous keeping of the Law. Our only true hope was to be found in Christ and to be saved "through faith in Christ" (3:9). Right standing with God can only come from God. And it can only come by means of our trust in what God has done through Christ.

How does faith in Christ provide the kind of righteousness we need before God?

"One life to live will soon be past, only what's done for Christ will last."
—JIM ELLIOT

EXPLORE

We can accumulate all sorts of human accomplishments in a lifetime. We can earn much money, win many awards, write many books, give all we possess to the poor, or "speak in the tongues of men and of angels" (1 Cor. 13:1–3). We can pastor a church, be on the church board, indeed, we can be a major denominational or international Christian figure. None of these things have any ultimate value in light of eternity. Even our goodness in this world is nothing when we stand before God. The only thing that matters in eternity is our ongoing trust in God and Jesus.

What are some of the things people typically value in themselves but are worth nothing when we stand before our king?

PRAYER

Jesus, thank you for your obedience to the point of death on a cross. Help me to see clearly how little I am next to your greatness.

DAY 4

LOOKING TOWARD RESURRECTION
Philippians 3:10-12

INTRODUCTION

Paul clearly stated the primary goals of his earthly life. In addition to knowing and being found in Christ, Paul wanted to know the power of Christ's resurrection. It was something he was not yet guaranteed, but something he pressed to make his own.

ENGAGE

It is understandable that Paul would think of himself as participating in the sufferings of Jesus. He was in prison as he wrote. Unlike his earlier letters, in Philippians, Paul seemed to sense he would die before Christ returned from heaven. Everything we know about his earthly ministry indicates it involved immense effort and faithfulness because of the opposition he faced from inside and outside the church. In such circumstances, priorities became very clear. Paul saw exactly where he was headed. He wanted to know Christ and the power of his resurrection, and the only path to get there was through suffering. So he pressed to reach the goal, and to take hold of it.

> "I do not run like a man running aimlessly; I do not fight like a man beating the air. No, I beat my body and make it my slave so that after I have preached to others, I myself will not be disqualified for the prize."
> —1 CORINTHIANS 9:26–27

EXAMINE

I have intentionally chosen verses today that cut across the paragraph division in the NIV so that you can see the context of what Paul says in 3:12. Too often, this verse is ripped from its context and misread as if Paul said he was not perfect but was trying to get better. But it is clear from the preceding verse that Paul was talking about resurrection. The New Revised Standard Version puts it this way: "Not that I have already obtained this [assurance of resurrection] or have already reached the goal; but I press on to make it my own, because Christ Jesus has made me his own." Paul wrote similarly in 3:14 of the "heavenward" call for which he was pressing on. As in 1 Corinthians 9:26–27, Paul expressed his need to continue striving in faithfulness until the end.

What do you think it means in real life to know the power of Jesus' resurrection?

EXPLORE

We must start where these verses end: Christ has first laid hold of us. We must always bear this fact in mind before we talk about our part in salvation or the necessity of faithfulness in this life. And it not only begins with Christ, but it is only after we are found in Christ that our efforts matter at all. Now, empowered by the Holy Spirit, we must strive. We must participate in Christ's sufferings, in whatever difficulties we might face in our pilgrimage of faithfulness. The goal is resurrection, the upward call. Christians are not guaranteed the resurrection despite how admirably they start the journey. We must go the whole way if we are to attain the resurrection of the dead.

What are some evidences that you are pressing toward the goal? Where might you need to press harder or more consistently?

PRAYER

Father, thank you for the work you have done for me in Christ, for taking hold of me, for offering Christ for me, and for raising Jesus from the dead.

PRESSING ON
Philippians 3:13-16

INTRODUCTION

It is finally in these verses that Paul got to the topic so many assume the whole passage is about: growing as believers. Paul reiterated the goal he had mentioned repeatedly—the prize of resurrection. Then he urged the Philippians to move forward toward it without losing ground.

ENGAGE

These particular verses end with a snapshot of a mature Christian—someone who recognizes that what is really important is not what is behind, but what is ahead. What Paul did before A.D. 33, when he believed in Christ, was now irrelevant in light of eternity both in terms of his accomplishments and his failures, but he could not simply rest on his conversion either. He needed to keep pressing on for the goal.

The New American Standard Bible probably translates 3:14 better when it speaks of the "prize of the upward call of God in Christ Jesus." Sure, Paul would still have moments of failure, but he was pressing on and headed in the right direction.

EXAMINE

Paul played on Greek words for *perfect* in these verses. In English, this word has taken on a sense of absolute perfection—no fault or error whatsoever. This meaning is so far removed from anything the Bible ever meant. In 3:12, Paul said he had not yet "been made perfect" (*teleioo*) or, as another translation puts it, had not yet "reached the goal" (NRSV). In 3:15, Paul said as many as are "perfect" (*teleios*, a word the NIV rightly translates as "mature") should think as he did. These two verses capture the interplay between the degree to which Christians have arrived, as well as that for which they are striving.

In English, what are the differences between being perfect and being mature?

"I find the great thing in the world is not so much
where we stand, as in what direction we are moving."
—OLIVER WENDELL HOLMES, SR.

EXPLORE

This stretch of verses gives us a lovely picture of the past, present, and future of the Christian pilgrimage. Having listened to what Paul said, we can acknowledge that moving forward with Christ involves forgetting our past sins and failures, as well as our successes. Once we are forgiven, we can forget our pasts and focus on a present and future that is a matter of Christ. Our future is the upward call, the prize of resurrection. Our present is about being in Christ and walking in faithfulness with him. This mature perspective moves forward in faith, being careful not to lose ground.

How can (and should) our future direct the course of our present?

PRAYER

Lead on, O eternal King. May my past successes and failures fade from view. May I ever progress toward your kingdom. May I never lose ground.

BRIDGING PAUL'S WORLD AND OURS

There is something about humans that makes us want to have heroes. For whatever reason, we tend to idolize others. We make them embody characteristics we wish we had. And usually, if we idealize them long enough, we will find out we were more infatuated with an idea than a reality. It happens time and time again in the news, as yet another actor, politician, or Christian figure disappoints us. Sometimes it is not a moral failure. Sometimes we just see their ordinariness and understand that they are really just like us.

One thing we learn from Philippians 3 is that most of this idealization is looking in the wrong direction in the first place. The earthly things we tend to look at—strength, intelligence, wealth, social status—are not things worth our dreamy infatuation. We should have our minds set on heavenly matters, which does not just include getting to heaven or Christ's return. It means that we are living in this world with Christ always in view—his values, his way of living. We are living on earth as citizens of heaven and looking for how the kingdom of God might influence the earth through us.

EXERCISE

For the next twenty-four hours, pay attention to people either in real life, in the media, or even in fiction who immediately spark some admiration in you. Then ask yourself why they do. Are there people you should admire more than you do? People you should admire less?

FOLLOW MY EXAMPLE

Philippians 3:17–4:7

"Therefore, my brothers, you whom I love and long for, my joy and crown, that is how you should stand firm in the Lord, dear friends!"

—PHILIPPIANS 4:1

GUARD AGAINST CHRIST'S ENEMIES

Philippians 3:17-19

INTRODUCTION

Paul finished chapter 3 by returning to his warnings from the beginning of the chapter against Christians who insist on circumcision. Such Christians, who focused on matters of eating and earthly things, ironically, were enemies of the cross of Christ.

ENGAGE

Paul considered the focus of other Christians on issues like whether Gentiles needed to be circumcised or whether Jewish and Gentile believers could eat together as setting your mind "on earthly things" (3:19). It was to glory in one's skin or stomach, an orientation that, in reality, reflected shameful attitudes toward the body of Christ. We do not debate these issues today, so Paul's position seems obvious to us.

Of course God would accept an uncircumcised man. Of course we can eat together regardless of where your meat came from or how it was prepared. But these are issues of the Old Testament, and time has afforded clarity that the New Testament believers were not blessed with.

EXAMINE

Scholars debate whether Paul was talking about Judaizing Christians in these verses—Christians who insisted you had to become a Jew to be saved—or about Jewish opponents to Christianity in general. It is heart-wrenching to think that Paul would say that other believers were enemies of the cross destined for destruction. Nevertheless, since the chapter likely begins with such Judaizers in mind, Paul probably had them in mind here as well. He called these individuals "false brothers" in Galatians 2:4. The comment that "their god is their stomach" (Phil. 3:19) might easily relate to issues of Jewish and Gentile Christians eating together at the table, an issue that Paul fought over and probably lost at Antioch (see Gal. 2:12–13).

Why do you think Paul was so relentless in the way he described these Christians who also wanted to require people to follow the Law?

"If their purpose or activity is of human origin, it will fail.
But if it is from God, you will not be able to stop these men;
you will only find yourselves fighting against God."
—ACTS 5:38–39

EXPLORE

It is deeply ironic, yet discouragingly common, that Christians can be zealous in the name of God for things not central to the gospel. What is even more startling is that we often hide behind the Bible to do it. On Paul's issues, we know the right answers because his positions were recorded in Scripture. Whatever power or influence his opponents might have had at the time, the Holy Spirit did not empower their thoughts to persist either in the Scriptures or through the course of time. These observations should lead us to humility because our thoughts are unique within the history of the church. God always knows which position he favors—and he gets his church there in his own time.

How can a Christian remained convinced of an opinion on a certain topic yet hold the position in humility?

PRAYER

Spirit, give me a heart that is firm in what I believe but humble about the limits of my understanding. Help me to trust in your steering of history.

HEAVENLY CITIZENS
Philippians 3:20-21

INTRODUCTION

Unlike those whose mind is set on earthly things, Paul reminded the Philippians that their citizenship was in heaven. Because of this promise, Christians eagerly await Jesus' return, when we will transform our earthly bodies to be like his heavenly body.

ENGAGE

After Paul accused his Christian opponents for their earthly focus, he clarified that the citizenship of the true believer was in heaven. The city of Philippi was a Roman colony, so Paul's message that their true citizenship was in heaven would have had special meaning for them. It is possible that many, if any, of the Philippian Christians themselves would have been citizens of Philippi, a privilege not everyone who lived

there would have enjoyed. But they would have understood the image—
they should have drawn their identity not from physical things like eating,
but from the spiritual things of heaven, where Christ is and from where
he will one day return.

EXAMINE

It might be surprising to hear that our transformed, resurrected
bodies will be of the same sort as the resurrected body of Jesus. But Paul
mentioned this destiny for our bodies more than once (see 1 Cor. 15:49).
It is easy for us to focus so much on Jesus' divinity that we forget he was
fully human as well. Indeed, the New Testament talks more in terms of
his humanity than his divinity. The book of Hebrews says that he was
made like us in every way (2:17), except that he was without sin (4:15).
Just as his earthly body was exactly like ours, so the body we will
receive at the resurrection will be exactly like his resurrected body.

How does the biblical teaching about our resurrected bodies differ
from the way we typically think of life after death?

"All these people were still living by faith when they died . . .
they admitted that they were aliens and strangers on earth.
People who say such things show that they are looking for a
country of their own . . . a better country—a heavenly one."

—HEBREWS 11:13–14, 16

EXPLORE

It is a tricky thing to recognize that our primary identity is bound with heaven without minimizing the importance of living fully now on earth. When we go through a time of intense social persecution or personal crisis, it is understandable that our language tends to look to the age to come and the world beyond. Certainly our most essential and fundamental identity, as well as our final goal, is a function of heaven. However, our bodies are not evil, and God wishes us to be agents for good in this world as well. We cannot let our final destiny undermine our role as stewards of everything within our influence in this world.

What do you think it looks like to have your heart set on heaven while living fully on earth in the present?

PRAYER

Spirit, impress on me where my true identity lies without letting me forget that I am here in my current body today. Give me heavenly values to do earthly good.

DAY 3

STANDING FIRM
Philippians 4:1

INTRODUCTION

Paul summed up everything he said in Philippians 3 with the exhortation to "stand firm" (4:1), also reaffirming how much he loved and longed for them. They were his joy, and they would be his "crown" of reward on the day of Christ.

ENGAGE

Although much of Philippians 3 is autobiographical, the chapter begins and ends with warnings not to listen to those who insisted Gentiles must fully convert to Judaism to be saved or who insisted certain purity rules be followed if Jew and Gentile were to eat together. In the process of these warnings, Paul clarified the priority of heavenly things over these earthly ones. He focused on the goal of resurrection. Finally, at the end, he summarized it all—stand firm. He made this final plea in very affectionate terms. He mentioned how much they meant to him "whom [he] love[d]" and "dear friends" and said they were "long[ed] for" all in the space of one verse (4:1).

"After you have done everything, to stand. Stand firm then."
—EPHESIANS 6:13–14

EXAMINE

Crowns were rewards given in ancient athletic contexts. In such events, the Greeks did not have medals for gold, silver, and bronze. Only the winner received a crown, which was made from leaves. When Paul called the Philippians his "joy and crown" (4:1), he was likely returning to a theme we saw back in 2:16, where Paul hoped to be able to boast about the Philippians on the day of Christ. They represented for Paul a truly meaningful success in his life, a success for and through Christ. They were also his joy, a theme seen in every chapter of Philippians at least once (see 1:4, 18; 2:2, 18; 3:1; 4:1).

Do you think the church today often experiences the kind of love and joy expressed by Paul? Why or why not?

EXPLORE

How wonderful it would be if Christian leaders today truly thought of those within their care as beloved and longed for. To be sure, the meaning of these terms of affection in Paul's world might turn out to be somewhat different in ours. Our deepened sense of love and affection today are true for who we are and a key part of our interrelationships and actions. Christian leaders today should model themselves on Paul's words here in all these respects.

What does genuine love look like today in the context of Christian community?

PRAYER

Lord, empower me to love in my leading and being led. Above all, I ask you to lead me in the way you want me to go.

DAY 4

STOP BICKERING

Philippians 4:2-3

INTRODUCTION

Apparently, one of the points of disunity among the Philippians was an ongoing argument between two of Paul's coworkers in the church: Euodia and Syntyche. Paul encouraged his "loyal yokefellow" (4:3) to help them settle their differences.

ENGAGE

The theme of unity appears once again in these verses. Indeed, perhaps this particular conflict, more than any other, stands behind Paul's earlier admonitions to unity in 1:27—2:16. Given the names Paul listed here and elsewhere (see Rom. 16), there is every reason to believe that Paul's churches included both female and male leaders, and that all leaders ministered both to men and women in the community.

Paul said that the names of all these workers were in the "book of life," the only mention of such a book in all Paul's writings (Phil. 4:3). It is a metaphor for those who are going to be saved to eternal life.

EXAMINE

As is often the case, a local problem chanced to give us some of the names of key Christians in one of Paul's churches. We already know Epaphroditus from earlier in the letter. Here, Paul mentioned at least three other leaders in the church. First, he mentioned the two women having some sort of conflict: Euodia and Syntyche. He also mentioned Clement. Finally, he addressed someone as a "loyal yokefellow" (4:3), presumably a major leader in the church who might help the two women settle their differences. It is possible that the word translated "loyal yokefellow" (*syzygos*) is actually someone's name, Syzygos. However, church tradition holds that Paul was addressing Epaphroditus, who delivered the letter to Philippi.

What does Paul's willingness to publicly admonish people engaged in conflict tell you about his concern for unity in the church?

EXPLORE

It is an interesting phenomenon with religions that later generations often forget the reasons for rules and end up making them an end in and of themselves. For example, orthodox Jews today will not eat meat and milk together in the same meal because Exodus 23:19 says not to boil a young goat in its mother's milk. But this contemporary Jewish practice almost certainly has nothing to do with the original purpose of this prohibition. In the same way, some today set up artificial boundaries for what women can and cannot do in the church. One important takeaway from these verses is that Paul's ministry was much more flexible—women and men ministered in his churches as God opened the doors and used them.

How was Paul's attitude toward women in ministry a reflection of his overall understanding of the gospel?

"The gospel of Jesus Christ . . . knows no distinction of race, condition, or sex, therefore, no person evidently called of God to the gospel ministry, and duly qualified for it, should be refused ordination on account of race, condition, or sex."
—B. T. ROBERTS

PRAYER

Spirit, soften my heart whenever I put my own ideas above unity. Keep me from myself when I am quenching your work in my church community.

REJOICE!

Philippians 4:4-7

INTRODUCTION

The closing chapter of Philippians is filled with exhortations about peace and contentment in troubling times. In these verses, Paul encouraged the Philippians to rejoice and show their kindness to all. Then God would give them peace in their hearts and minds.

ENGAGE

The exhortations of these verses probably connect to each other, but each one is also valid in its own right. Rejoice, which Paul emphasized by repeating it twice. Be kind and gentle to others—be someone easy to get along with. Live in the expectation that Christ might return any day. Do not be anxious. God is in control. Bring your requests to God with an attitude of thanksgiving, and God will give you peace. It is a peace that transcends your situation, peace of heart, and mind despite your external circumstances. These are opportunities for the believer, often impossible in human power, but quite possible with God.

EXAMINE

Although Paul did not say so explicitly, he probably wrote these verses to address a time of tension and anxiety within the church. Paul seemed to have left out the key connecting words that could make the situation clearer for us. The Philippians should let others see their gentleness, being strengthened to do it because they know the Lord is at hand. In other words, hang in there and be careful not to give anyone an excuse to have cause against them. They were to present their situations to God and therefore not have any reason to be anxious, because they would have the peace of God. And so they would be able to rejoice in the Lord always, even in hard times.

How does it help your understanding of these verses to consider the probable context of them?

EXPLORE

Most Sunday school children know the song, "Rejoice in the Lord always, and again I say, rejoice." The words may be so familiar to us that we read right past them. Christians are supposed to be people of joy. And we should not only be people of joy when times are pleasurable. After all, Paul did not write Philippians during a time of prosperity for him. It is a peace beyond understanding because it is not a peace we might expect to have. It is a peace in the middle of a storm. It is not peace of the body, but rather peace of the heart and mind. And surely God would not offer it if he did not intend to give it.

For what situations or circumstances do you need to experience God's peace today?

"Joy is a net of love by which you can catch souls."
—MOTHER TERESA

PRAYER

Father, I give thanks for your promise of peace. Free my heart and mind from the slavery of fear and anxiety so that I can rejoice instead.

BRIDGING PAUL'S WORLD AND OURS

The words of James 3:2 about the difficulty of taming the tongue ring true. We all know how hard it is to reel words back in once they have left our mouths. True, there are those who have thick skins—you can say almost anything to them and they seem unaffected. But most of us get wounded pretty easily with words.

On the whole, the Philippian church seems to have been one of Paul's least problematic. We do not find any letters to them in the New Testament like those of Galatians or 1 Corinthians, both of which contain major correction. But even this seemingly harmonious church had its moments, such as the squabble between Euodia and Syntyche. There is little doubt that all churches have slight disagreements from time to time.

Some people have learned to put a five minute delay on their outgoing e-mail; some put more. That little delay can mean the difference between harmony and catastrophe. Think what a difference it would make if we could put one of those on our mouths—or on our hands and feet. What a great discipline: the discipline of delay.

EXERCISE

Put a delay on your mouth and body for the next twenty-four hours. You decide how long—five seconds, ten seconds. Whenever you are about to say or do something with potential impact, hit the pause button. At the end of the day, reflect on the effect it has had.

REJOICING IN GIFTS

Philippians 4:8-23

"Yet it was good of you to share in my troubles. . . .
And my God will meet all your needs according
to his glorious riches in Christ Jesus."

—PHILIPPIANS 4:14, 19

THINKING VIRTUES

Philippians 4:8-9

INTRODUCTION

Paul gave a list of virtuous things that are what believers should think about—whatever is true, noble, right, pure, lovely, admirable, excellent, or praiseworthy. These are the sorts of things, Paul said, that the Philippians had received and heard from him.

ENGAGE

Virtue lists, of the sort Paul gave here, were common among ancient philosophers. Paul mentioned six excellent and praiseworthy virtues on which a Christian should focus. Virtuous people think on things that are true, where truth is something more than logic. It is to be aligned with God and his reality. What is noble and just has to do with the kinds of actions God values. It involves righting the oppressed and helping the un-empowered. Pure, lovely, and admirable things are things that God approves of, things that please him. So all these virtues mean that a person is doing the things that fit with who God is and what he wants.

EXAMINE

Although we are looking at these verses by themselves, they probably go better with the verses we looked at last week. A train of thought that started with Paul telling the Philippians to imitate him (3:17) ended here with Paul asking them again to do the things they had heard him say and seen him do. The result would be that "the God of peace [would] be with [them]" (4:9), a statement that reminds us of the peace beyond understanding just a couple of verses before. Paul's confidence can be startling to us. He was confident that his teaching was right and his life was blameless before God. Indeed, he implied that his ministry exemplified these sorts of virtues.

What do these verses imply about the relationship between our thoughts and actions?

EXPLORE

What we put in front of us can have a profound effect on our minds. Our brains have cells called "mirror cells." These cells, in effect, replay in our minds what we see. If we see a murder in a movie, these cells reenact the murder in our minds. The end result is that what we look at—including things like pornography and violence—make a significant impact on who we are. It is very difficult in the Western world today to get away from the constant raping of our minds by what we see, so we must do all we can to expose our minds to things that are virtuous.

How can Christians most effectively train their minds to focus on the things Paul recommended?

"O be careful little eyes what you see . . . O be careful little ears what you hear . . . O be careful little hands what you do . . ."
—"O BE CAREFUL, LITTLE EYES"

PRAYER

Father, keep the true, noble, and pure before my eyes, and give me the strength to shield my eyes from the barrage of the false, ignoble, and impure around me.

REJOICING IN GIVING

Philippians 4:10-13

INTRODUCTION

Paul rejoiced tactfully in the material support the Philippians brought to him by Epaphroditus, while making it clear that he had learned to be content, whether he had much or little. God taught him the secret to being content.

ENGAGE

Two profound verses of hope are nestled in this paragraph. The first is in 4:11, where Paul said he had "learned to be content whatever the circumstances." While others in his day (like the Stoics) argued that you should accept your fate, Paul's contentment was based on the Christian hope, not on a mere acceptance that everything happens for a reason. It was this hope that the Lord was near and would set the world straight that made it possible to be at peace regardless of his circumstances. The second is in 4:13, where Paul expressed his faith that he could do everything he had to through God's strength. What great promises Paul experienced and passed on to the people of God!

EXAMINE

In this passage and through verse 19, Paul walked a fine line through a social land mine. Receiving gifts in the ancient world had a tendency to establish obligations. Interestingly, Paul never thanked the Philippians for their aid in these verses. Rather, he rejoiced in the fact that they had been able to fulfill their desire to help him. He did not admit to having need, which might have set up the web of obligation that could exist with giver-recipient relationships. Instead, Paul learned the secret of contentment regardless of his material circumstances, since it was God who truly gave him what he needed to keep going and do what needed to be done.

What or who was the source of Paul's contentment, and how did it develop within him?

EXPLORE

We have seen the theme of peace and contentment in hard times throughout Philippians. We saw it as Paul contemplated death in chapter 1. We have seen it in chapter 4 as Paul spoke about the peace that passes understanding. Paul went so far as to say he really did not have material need, and what needs he had were provided for by God. Could we ever develop this perspective, with God's grace? Imagine being content no matter our circumstances because we trusted God for our needs today and to resolve all things in the end. Imagine thinking about giving as returning our obligation to God rather than our service to others.

How can you practice contentment in your own life?

"It is better to want what you have than
to have what you want."

—AUTHOR UNKNOWN

PRAYER

Father, thank you for the gifts you give all the time, even when my need is not clear to me. May all my service to others be thankfulness to you.

REMEMBERING GENEROSITY

Philippians 4:14-17

INTRODUCTION

Paul remembered the history of the aid the Philippians had given him over the years since the beginning of his ministry to them. He praised them for doing good in these respects and considered their generosity something God would credit to them.

ENGAGE

As we saw yesterday, Paul was walking a fine line in this last part of the letter. He did not directly thank the Philippians for their gift. Rather, he said they did well to share in his trials. He denied that he was seeking such support. What he sought was to see them grow, to see the fruit multiplied to their credit. Giving was therefore something that was important for them rather than for Paul. The implication is that our giving to others is a sign of our growth. Giving is something we should expect of mature believers. It is to the Philippians' credit, but it is not something over and above the call of duty.

EXAMINE

As often happens, we learn some details of Paul's ministry from the seemingly incidental comments he made. For example, we find out that the Philippian church supported Paul materially at least twice while he was in Thessalonica (Phil. 4:15–16). This brief mention suggests Paul was in Thessalonica a little bit longer than one might think from the narrative of Acts alone (see Acts 17:1–9). The comment also fills out our sense of Paul's policy on receiving assistance. He apparently did not receive help from a church while he was present in its city (see 2 Cor. 11:8–9). He probably did not want to accept the kind of obligation that went along with receiving gifts. But once he had left a city, then he might have accepted assistance.

Why do you think Paul thought of the Philippians' gifts to him as "shar[ing] in [his] troubles" (Phil. 4:14)?

EXPLORE

Westerners can have such a highly developed sense of personal property that we can think our giving makes us saints. Quite the contrary; everything we have belongs to God, and sharing from our excess is part of thanking God for sharing with us what is ultimately his. This passage can be a significant check on our perspective in giving. Sharing in the troubles of others with our material resources is the kind of fruit God expects of his people. Giving is "credited to [our] account" (4:17), but not giving is not neutral to God's reckoning. Not giving goes against our account.

How can Christians today learn and practice their ability to share in the sufferings of others by giving to them out of their plenty?

"Make all you can, save all you can, give all you can."
—JOHN WESLEY

PRAYER

Father, help me to see my giving to others as a service to you. Teach me to see my possessions as yours rather than seeing them as my own.

GOD MEETS NEEDS
Philippians 4:18-20

INTRODUCTION

Paul told of the abundance and fullness he enjoyed because of the Philippians' faithfulness, but he spoke of their gifts as offerings to God. He assured them that God would supply any needs they might have in the future, just as God had supplied all of Paul's needs.

ENGAGE

With these verses, Paul brought the body of the letter to a close, ending it on a high note of praise to our God and Father. He continued to put the Philippians' gifts to him in the context of what they owed God rather than something they were doing for him. This leads to another wonderful promise—that God supplies his people's needs. The bank from which God draws this support is the wealth that is in Jesus.

God met Paul's needs—he received a "full payment and even more" (4:18). And God met the Philippians' needs.

EXAMINE

This is the second time Paul used the image of the Philippians' faithfulness as a kind of sacrifice offered to God. The first time was in 2:17, where Paul likened his sufferings to a drink offering poured out on the Philippians' own sacrifice in faithfulness. Here, Paul compared their material support to a sacrifice pleasing to God. The brilliance of this imagery is that it seems to picture their giving to Paul as their response to God's gifts and patronage to them. God is the one who, as the divine giver of perfect gifts, supplied their needs. Their gifts to Paul were not them serving as his patrons, but returning thanks to God for his unmerited favor.

How could Paul say that he was not in need (4:11) then say that the Philippians' gifts provided everything he needed (4:18)?

EXPLORE

We do not need most of the things we think we do. Parents often experience the difficulty of teaching their children to distinguish between their needs and wants. Adults can be just as bad—only we do not have someone with parental authority to correct us. We need those clothes, or we need that car. Probably the greatest value is when we are able to see ourselves and our assumptions. When we have seen how most of the world lives, as on a mission trip, it is hard to think we have much true need of anything more.

What helps you to distinguish between the needs and the wants in your life? How can you practice discernment in this area?

"God loves a cheerful giver."
—2 CORINTHIANS 9:7

PRAYER

Jesus, thank you for supplying every true need I have. Help me to see the difference between what I want and what I need.

FAREWELL GREETINGS
Philippians 4:21-23

INTRODUCTION

Paul closed this letter with typical greetings from him and those with him, and he wished God's grace on the spirit of all in the community.

ENGAGE

From Philippians and elsewhere we know that Paul thought of the community of faith everywhere as a family, a household. Those with him were brothers and sisters. Apparently, a number of those who worked for the Roman government came to believe, possibly from Paul's own witness while he was imprisoned. Although they still worked for Caesar and were in his household (slaves and other employees were considered part of a household), they were also now in the household of God—citizens of heaven. Meanwhile, the Philippians were "saints"

(4:21) or holy ones. They were God's possession, set apart for him, electrified by the connection with his Spirit.

"Thou our Father, Christ our Brother, all who live in love are Thine.
Teach us how to love each other, lift us to the Joy Divine."
—HENRY VAN DYKE

EXAMINE

Mention of Caesar's household supports the tradition that Paul was imprisoned in Rome as he wrote this letter. The "palace guard," mentioned in 1:13, also fits a Roman location. However, the empire had such palace headquarters in other locations too, including Jerusalem (see Mark 15:16), and Caesar's household included the entire Roman administrative system scattered throughout the world. In the end, I have favored Ephesus as the place from which Paul wrote Philippians. It fits better with his future travel plans. It fits with the visits and news relating to Epaphroditus, since Ephesus was much closer than Rome for such communication. It fits the general circumstances Paul alluded to in 2 Corinthians 1:8.

Do you think these verses are a mere formality, or do they represent an example for us to follow? If they are an example, how does the example instruct us?

EXPLORE

Christian fellowship is not some optional, side aspect of church life. It is a central feature, perhaps even more important than having perfect understanding. How few congregations—let alone groups of churches—think of themselves as a family! One trend is toward non-denominational, self-standing churches that are not governed by any church hierarchy. One potential down side is a loss of fellowship between churches, of the family relationship Paul tried to foster between his churches. One practice we might consider developing is viewing each other as God's possession or holy, including other churches. Maybe we would treat each other a little differently if we saw God when we looked at one another. All of this requires God's grace, which thankfully he is eager to give.

How do you think churches would network differently if they had a deep understanding of God's desire for family unity in the church?

PRAYER

Jesus Christ, whom Scripture describes as my brother, mend your people into a true family that loves each individual completely and is filled with grace.

BRIDGING PAUL'S WORLD AND OURS

John Wesley famously said, "Make all you can, save all you can, give all you can." By saving, he was not advocating putting money away in the bank. Instead, he meant not to spend more than you had.

We do not live in the New Testament world—those who rarely entertained the idea that everyone could be wealthy. They generally categorized the rich as thieves. The goal was to have what you needed to survive and to give to those in need anything extra you might have.

Few people in the Western world live this way—giving until it hurts—but perhaps this is just what Paul is calling us to do.

EXERCISE

For the next twenty-four hours, pay special attention to everything you buy or don't buy. Which of your purchases do you really need to survive? Calculate how much you spend in a day that could go toward others in greater need.

Life Lessons from the Apostle to the Nations

Who was this Paul, long-ago tentmaker and missionary, and what does his life and writings have to teach us today? Author Kenneth Schenck bridges time and culture to bring you *Paul—Messenger of Grace*. Immerse yourself in the world of one of history's most polarizing figures to learn from his background, conversion, missionary journeys, and letters. *Paul—Messenger of Grace* covers the earlier part of Paul's life and ministry including 1 Thessalonians, 1 and 2 Corinthians, Galatians, and Philippians.

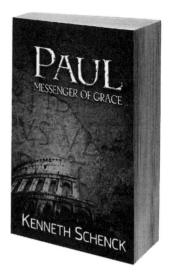

Paul—Messenger of Grace
Kenneth Schenck

Price: $14.99
ISBN: 978-0-89827-439-4

Apply Paul's Teaching to Everyday Life
Messenger of Grace Bible Studies

The *Messenger of Grace* Bible Study series, based on Kenneth Schenck's *Paul—Messenger of Grace*, helps small groups and individuals go deeper in their understanding of Paul's life and letters while helping them apply that understanding into their daily lives. Each six-week study focuses on one of Paul's letters from the earlier part of his ministry and includes both weekly and daily study components.

Our Hope: 1 Thessalonians
Our Joy: Philippians
Kenneth Schenck

Price: $7.99
ISBN: *Our Hope* 978-0-89827-441-7
   Our Joy 978-0-89827-442-4

wesleyan
publishing
house

www.wesleyan.org/wph or call toll free
1.800.493.7539 M–F 8 a.m.–4:30 p.m. ET

Life Lessons from Paul's Later Letters

Paul went from persecuting the Jewish Christians to battling the principalities and powers so that he could extend their Christian faith throughout the Greco-Roman world. Author Kenneth Schenck delivers more than a narrative recounting of history. Each chapter concludes with the author's insightful reflections of how Paul's life and letters can shape our lives more into the image of Christ. *Paul—Soldier of Peace* covers the later part of Paul's life and ministry including the letters of Romans, Ephesians, Colossians, 2 Thessalonians, 1 and 2 Timothy, and Titus.

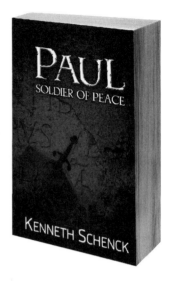

Paul—Soldier of Peace
Kenneth Schenck
Price: $14.99
ISBN: 978-0-89827-440-0

Apply Paul's Teaching to Everyday Life
Soldier of Peace Bible Studies

In the *Soldier of Peace* Bible Study series, based on Kenneth Schenck's *Paul—Soldier of Peace*, Schenck brings both understanding and practical application of Paul's life and letters to readers today. These six-week studies focus on Paul's letters from the later part of his ministry and include both weekly and daily study components.

Our Righteousness: Romans 1–8
Our Relationships: Romans 9–16
Kenneth Schenck
Price: $7.99
ISBN: Our Righteousness 978-0-89827-443-1
　　　　Our Relationships 978-0-89827-444-8

wesleyan
publishing
house

www.wesleyan.org/wph or call toll free
1.800.493.7539 M–F 8 a.m.–4:30 p.m. ET

Hear God's Word for Yourself!

God said it; I believe it; that settles it for me! The spirit with which someone might make that statement is often right on target. When we know God's will on a particular issue, no human reason can—or should—change our minds. Yet not every issue is that clear-cut. The average Christian is awash in conflicting ideas about what the Bible means. Many people feel inadequate to pick up a Bible, read, and understand it for themselves. Kenneth Schenck's *Making Sense of God's Word* offers practical help for the average Christian who wants to read God's Word and understand it. Helping the reader sort through the issues of context, genre, and theories of interpretation, Schenck gives practical principles that restore confidence in reading and interpreting Scripture. After reading this simple, practical guide, readers will feel confident that they can "hear God's Word" for themselves.

Making Sense of God's Word
Kenneth Schenck

Price: $9.99
ISBN: 978-0-89827-376-2

wesleyan
publishing
house

www.wesleyan.org/wph or call toll free
1.800.493.7539 M–F 8 a.m.–4:30 p.m. ET

Read with Understanding!

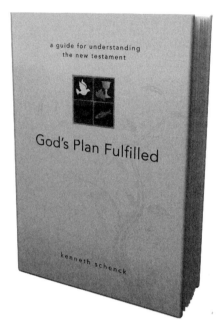

Many people want to read the Bible but have trouble knowing where to begin and making sense of what they are reading. *God's Plan Fulfilled* is a concise introduction to the New Testament that makes God's Word accessible to the average reader. Opening chapters give the reader an overview of the content of the New Testament. Author Kenneth Schenck then guides the reader through each book of the New Testament, offering background information, an overview of the content, and specific help for understanding key events, ideas, and passages. Each chapter includes sidebars that enhance understanding and key information such as "big ideas" and themes for clarification. Questions for application and discussion are included.

God's Plan Fulfilled: A Guide for Understanding the New Testament
Kenneth Schenck

Price: $19.99
ISBN: 978-0-89827-378-6

wesleyan
publishing
house

www.wesleyan.org/wph or call toll free
1.800.493.7539 M–F 8 a.m.–4:30 p.m. ET